AMICUS ILLUSTRATED • AMICUS INK

DO YOU REALLY WANT TO MEET
AN ANTEATER?

WRITTEN BY CARI MEISTER   ILLUSTRATED BY DANIELE FABBRI

Amicus Illustrated and Amicus Ink
are published by Amicus
P.O. Box 1329
Mankato, MN 56002
www.amicuspublishing.us

Library of Congress Cataloging-in-Publication Data
Names: Meister, Cari, author. | Fabbri, Daniele, illustrator.
Title: Do you really want to meet an anteater? / by Cari
    Meister ; illustrated by Daniele Fabbri.
Description: Mankato, Minnesota : Amicus Illustrated/
    Amicus Ink, [2019] | Series: Amicus. Do you really
    want to meet...? | Audience: K to grade 3. | Includes
    bibliographical references.
Identifiers: LCCN 2017039247 (print) | LCCN
    2017049883 (ebook) | ISBN 9781681514765 (pdf)
    | ISBN 9781681513942 (library binding) | ISBN
    9781681523149 (pbk.)
Subjects: LCSH: Myrmecophaga-Juvenile literature. |
    CYAC: Anteaters.
Classification: LCC QL737.E24 (ebook) | LCC QL737.
    E24 M45 2019 (print) | DDC 599.3/14-dc23
LC record available at https://lccn.loc.gov/2017039247

Editor: Rebecca Glaser
Designer: Kathleen Petelinsek

Printed in the United States of America

HC 10 9 8 7 6 5 4 3 2 1
PB 10 9 8 7 6 5 4 3 2 1

ABOUT THE AUTHOR

Cari Meister has written more than 200 books for children,
including the TINY series (Viking), and the FAIRY HILL
series (Scholastic). She lives in Edwards, Colorado, with
her husband, four sons, a goldendoodle named Koki, and
an Arabian horse named Sir William. Find out more at
carimeister.com.

ABOUT THE ILLUSTRATOR

Daniele Fabbri was born in Ravenna, Italy, in 1978. He
graduated from Istituto Europeo di Design in Milan, Italy,
and started his career as a cartoon animator, storyboarder,
and background designer for animated series. He has
worked as a freelance illustrator since 2003, collaborating
with advertising agencies and international publishers, and
has illustrated many books for Amicus.

What's that odd-looking creature with the long nose and fluffy tail?

It's a giant anteater!
That long snout helps vacuum
in about 30,000 ants a day!
What's that? You want to meet
an anteater in the wild?

CLAWS

4 incheS

It's true that an anteater doesn't have teeth. And it can't see well. But an anteater can be dangerous if it's cornered. It is as big as a golden retriever! And look at those claws. They are about 4 inches (10 cm) long and super sharp. They can tear through skin.

Do you *really* want to meet a giant anteater?

Yes?

Pack your stuff. You're off to Brazil.

Welcome! You're now in the
Pantanal—a protected wetland where
anteaters and many other animals live.

Your tour guide tells you that anteaters are not easy to find. They are shy. And there aren't as many as there used to be. Some of their habitat has been lost. Some anteaters are hunted or hit by cars.

You start looking for clues.
You know that giant anteaters
eat ants and termites. If you
find them, maybe you'll find
an anteater.

You spot a bunch of termite mounds.

Rustle. *Rustle*. What's that? Is it an anteater?

You peek through the tall grass. It's a tapir!
These strange animals with short trunks live here too.

Your tour group gets close to a water hole. Animals like
this capybara come here to drink, so you watch and wait.

Then you see a long, feathery tail. And a long
tube-shaped nose. It is a giant anteater!

The anteater drinks and then slowly walks toward a termite mound. He digs with his claws, tearing open the mound. He flicks his long tongue in and out, slurping up termites.

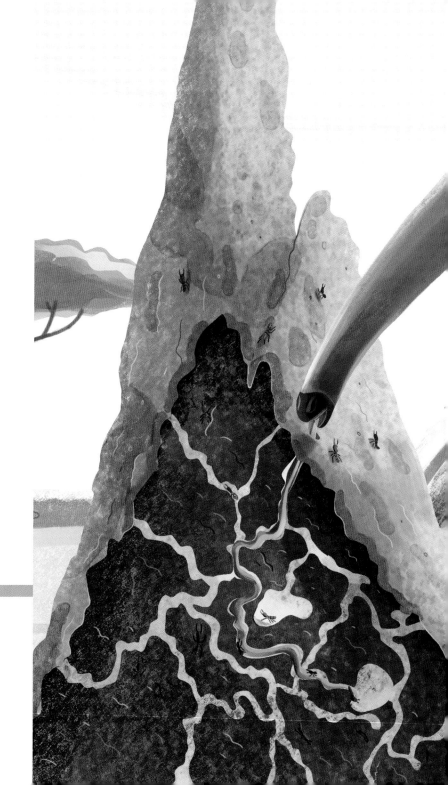

The giant anteater has the longest tongue in relation to its body of any mammal. It's almost 2 feet (60 cm) long. It can flick up to 150 times a minute!

But wait. What's that? It's a jaguar! Anteaters don't have many predators, but jaguars will attack them. The anteater stands up on his hind legs. He opens his arms. It looks like he wants a hug. But that's no friendly gesture. That's his warning pose. His giant claws are ready to strike.

The jaguar growls and bats a paw. The anteater lunges. His claws dig into flesh. The jaguar growls again and walks away.

Wow! Anteaters are powerful! And now
you've really seen an anteater in the wild.

WHERE DO GIANT ANTEATERS LIVE?

SOUTH AMERICA

MAP KEY

● Giant anteater range

GLOSSARY

Brazil A large country in South America.

capybara A large rodent that looks like a giant guinea pig and lives in South America.

Pantanal A very large tropical wetland in South America; parts of the Pantanal are protected so people don't disturb the environment and hunting is not allowed.

predator An animal that hunts and eats other animals.

tapir A pig-like animal with a short trunk and short legs.

termite An insect that eats wood and lives in a large group.

wetland An area of land that is covered with pools of water.

READ MORE

Calhoun, Kelly. *Sneaky Snouts.*
Ann Arbor, Mich.: Cherry Lake
Publishing, 2016.

Gillespie, Katie. **Giant Anteater.**
New York: AV2 by Weigl, 2017.

Ghinga, Charles, ed. **Animal Planet
Strange, Unusual, Gross, and Cool
Animals.** New York: Time Inc.
Books, 2016.

Snyder, Eleanor. *Angry Anteaters.*
New York: Gareth Stevens, 2016.

WEBSITES

Animal Planet: Giant Anteater
*http://www.animalplanet.com/wild-animals
/10-giant-anteater/*
Read more about the giant anteater.

ARKive: Giant Anteater
*http://www.arkive.org/giant-anteater
/myrmecophaga-tridactyla/*
Watch videos and see photos of giant anteaters in the wild.

San Diego Zoo: Giant Anteater
http://animals.sandiegozoo.org/animals/giant-anteater
Find basic facts about the giant Anteater here. Great site
for reports.

*Every effort has been made to ensure that these websites are appropriate for
children. However, because of the nature of the Internet, it is impossible to
guarantee that these sites will remain active indefinitely or that their contents
will not be altered.*